Daily Meditation Beginner's Guide From Happines & Good Life to Stress Release, Relaxation, Healing, Weight Loss & Zen

Juliana Baltimoore

Published by InfinitYou, 2017.

While every precaution has been taken in the preparation of this book, the publisher assumes no responsibility for errors or omissions, or for damages resulting from the use of the information contained herein.

DAILY MEDITATION BEGINNER'S GUIDE FROM HAPPINES & GOOD LIFE TO STRESS RELEASE, RELAXATION, HEALING, WEIGHT LOSS & ZEN

First edition. June 30, 2017.

Copyright © 2017 Juliana Baltimoore.

Written by Juliana Baltimoore.

Welcome

I welcome you to "The Daily Meditation Ritual Lifestyle".

This book is part of the "Daily Ritual Secret Series".

It is written by a true and passionate meditation practitioner who applies the proper and deep meditation ritual on a daily basis religiously.

My name is Alecandra Baldec and I welcome all of you to my own branded version of the meditation lifestyle.

I call my meditation lifestyle:

"The Daily Meditation Ritual Lifestyle"

I truly practice this daily meditation ritual myself.

Even if it is 2 pm in the morning and I have not been able to do my meditation before, I always find some creative and inspiring ways to never skip my daily meditation.

Soon you are going to find out for yourself how you can do this for yourself.

This book will show you exactly how you can find out your own daily meditation ritual lifestyle.

I have trained countless meditation students to become better meditators via my proper and deep daily meditation ritual and they have found out their proper meditation lifestyle that they truly enjoy every day.

Finally, I am a researcher and writer and love to find out the latest buzz, ideas, methods, and techniques about how to live a better lifestyle with meditation in mind.

In this book I will cover helpful and applicable meditation lifestyle advice for everyone who would love to lead a happy and healthy meditation lifestyle.

Have you noticed that books around the topic of how to meditate properly really have become hot topics over the last few years?

Yes, it is true meditation and especially new age type of meditation and guided meditation instructions have become very popular over the years.

This guide discusses the best and most popular meditation techniques and the goal is to go through all of them and choose the one that you like best.

Then go and apply it to your own daily meditation ritual.

The focus of the book is to create your own personal daily meditation ritual lifestyle.

Once you have found out what meditation technique you like the best, you will be able to achieve your own meditation ritual and you will be able to integrate it effortlessly into your daily lifestyle.

Once you have gone through my meditation ritual checklist and evaluation process, applying your own meditation ritual is becoming a very easy process.

Yes, it is going to become a very effortlessly process like breathing for example.

I have also included lots of tips for meditation beginners as well.

Advanced users on the other hand will learn how to reinforce and reevaluate their daily meditation routine, and they will be able to reestablish and solidify a very deep and proper meditation ritual.

Once you have gone through this guide, you probably will be able to see meditation from a different angle.

I am trying to provide you with a very actionable and user friendly guide and system that is very helpful for beginners who are starting out.

Advanced users can get a lot of new insights out of this guide and in conjunction with other meditation techniques.

Heck, why not mix and match some new insights from this guide with your meditation inventory.

You might even come up with some new hybrid forms of meditation. Be creative with this guide and think in terms of unlimited possibilities.

The guide will help you figure out the answers that you have in relation to the question how do I set up my daily meditation routine the right and proper way to achieve the ultimate mediation lifestyle that I enjoy and that makes me happy - every day!

Go ahead and get started with the guide and you will be able to achieve the ultimate mediation lifestyle for yourself.

This is the coolest lifestyle ever and if you have never before been able to reach this ultimate meditation lifestyle, then go start right now...

What Is Proper And Deep Meditation?

Proper and deep meditation is a mental exercise or ritual that if done the proper way has to be repeated on a daily basis.

When an individual is doing meditation the proper way, he or she is training the mind.

If done correctly, the meditator induces a mode of deep consciousness in order to achieve some mental, physical, and spiritual benefit.

There are many varieties of practicing meditation.

Meditation ranges from techniques that are designed to achieve great relaxation of the body and mind to other techniques that are building internal energy.

Other types of meditation methods are designed for contacting spiritual guides, receiving psychic visions, and spiritual experiences like getting closer to higher forces and powers.

Yet other types of meditation techniques are promoting things like seeing past life, taking an astral journey, and the like.

All of these meditation techniques have one common achievement in common and that is: love, patience, generosity, forgiveness and more far-reaching goals such as effortlessly sustained single-pointed concentration, single-pointed analysis, and an indestructible sense of well-being and this is what is called mindfulness.

In order to start your chosen meditation technique the proper and right way, you should be mindful about the meaning of meditation.

Let's look how does the dictionary define meditation? The dictionary defines the meditative process like this: "continued or extended thought; reflection; contemplation."

Interesting, but what does this mean for our reality and lifestyle?

As human beings we get overwhelmed on a daily basis. This overwhelm can lead to stressful situations with tension which in most of the cases can affect our health in a very negative way.

Using meditation on a daily basis gives our mind a chance to calm itself and adjust to the stressful lifestyle and problems that are part of our modern day to day life.

Usually, people meditate in a placid and calm room or space, free from distraction.

There are many different techniques of meditation. I will cover these in later chapters.

All the meditation methods do lead to the same place and that is peace of mind and a disease free body.

Simply put, meditation is the process of quieting our mind. If done in the proper way, your mind becomes calmer and calmer. The "internal dialogue" that is part of our thinking process becomes calmer and calmer as you progress and become a better meditator.

You start to move mentally to a more calm and peaceful place, once you have mastered proper and deep meditation.

Sometimes meditation is described as reaching a higher state of consciousness which in other religions is called spirituality.

In meditation we experience this state of higher consciousness because our mind is less cluttered and distracted and therefore we start to notice things that would normally pass our mind unnoticed.

For example, while doing our meditation we may tune in more to the sounds that surround us like urban traffic and people sound or more rural natural sounds like singing birds and running water of a river.

The Goals Of The Proper Meditation Ritual

So what exactly do we need to know in order to get started with the daily meditation ritual and what are the goals of such a ritual?

In order to do meditation the proper and deep way, you first must consider to live an organic lifestyle. You can also consider to include some yoga practices, relaxation techniques, as well as other related techniques that will guide you to a proper and deep daily meditation ritual .

The daily meditation practice will make it easier for you to transform your lifestyle because you will learn on a daily basis how to transform your thinking patterns.

Once you transform your thinking patterns, you will start noticing some major developments and improvements that will benefit your whole body and mind.

You will start noticing your body mind connection and you will be noticing that your whole behavioral system will change. Once you start noticing this change, you have achieved your goal or what meditation experts call a proper and deep meditation ritual.

So, let's explore some more benefits a proper and deep meditation process and what it can do for you. Once you know how to meditate in a proper and deep way, you can guide your body and mind to relaxation in a very quick and easy manner. You will be able to reform your thinking and your actions.

You are going to do this by evaluating your overall behavior system, your lifestyle, your habits and your experiences.

The process is going to be very simple once you know how to do the meditation work. If you are not used to meditation, you will need to get started with a few basic steps that are going to depend on the specific meditation technique that you are going to choose in the next few chapters.

You will also need to get started with a healthier lifestyle. Once you are going to apply a daily meditation ritual which is the goal of this guide, your way of thinking is going to be transformed and you will receive the benefits that come from this change.

You should always be mindful about the meaning of meditation and you should be aware of the success ingredients that need to be applied for each different meditation technique. If you are following the guide you will ultimately be able to achieve your own daily meditation ritual lifestyle.

So I hope by now you understand the main priority of this guide and I hope that I have answered the question how do I get started with the daily meditation ritual?

If you understand the goal of this guide, we can now move on to the next chapter and learn how we can go deeper into a meditative state.

How Do I Get Started With The Daily Meditation Ritual?

So here we go, let's learn how to achieve a proper and deep meditation ritual.

First things first, choose a time and a place where you will not be interrupted and disturbed for the duration of your daily meditation sessions. This is the basis for a proper and deep meditation ritual and you have to respect this rule on a daily basis.

You may decide to set aside 5 or 20 minutes (depending on your personal needs and situation) for your daily meditation ritual. This gives you enough time and especially if you are a meditation beginner this time frame is an ideal starting point.

Whatever works for you in terms of time is good - it's much better to spend a few minutes a day meditating than to put it off and not doing it at all. Always remember 5 minutes is better than nothing.

As you progress, you may decide that you are getting plenty of benefits with a daily meditation ritual and you might want to increase the amount of time that you are spending in the deep meditative state as you progress with your meditation. Once you have reached that level where you are an experienced meditator, it is ok to increase your daily meditation time.

If you feel experienced enough, your daily goal in terms of time should be to exercise at least two 15-20 minute meditation sessions and stick to it.

Meditation gurus like Deepak Chopra do confirm based on their own experience, research and work with clients that spending a minimum of 15-20 minutes a day leads to better health and a disease free life. It also can help reduce stress and reduce sleeping problems.

Checklist For A Daily Meditation Ritual

Check the following list and go through the rest of the guide based on this checklist in order to evaluate your personal situation.

Doing this evaluation work will help you find out which meditation technique you are going to choose for your daily meditation ritual.

Make sure to stick to this checklist and you will be able to achieve the ultimate meditation lifestyle and all the benefits that come with it:

- Choose one of the meditation methods from the following chapters
- Choose a time of day (morning, lunch, afternoon, evening) when you are not going to be interrupted. Make sure to repeat your meditation on a daily basis.
- Choose a placid place where you feel cosy, comfortable and where you can relax.
- If you do not have enough time to go through your chosen meditation method, replace your meditation method with the new age meditation technique.

You will be learning more about the new age meditation technique in the new age meditation chapter. Just do not skip ahead and come back to guideline number 4 once you have gone through the specific chapter that talks about new age meditation.

Learning the proper and deep meditation ritual is as easy as following these basic guidelines.

The time of day when you do your daily meditation ritual should be the same every day because this makes it easier for your body and brain to get used to this new habit and feeling.

Some meditators find that meditating early in the morning is the best time for them because no one is going to disturb them. Others like myself prefer to meditate last thing at night after a nice hot shower and a little work out and before going to sleep.

You may find that the best time for you is while the rest of your family is occupied with other things like watching TV. There is no perfect time that fits everyone. Whatever works for you is fine! Just make sure that you practice on a daily basis because otherwise you will never achieve a proper meditation lifestyle.

It is up to you to choose a place that you like and where you are going to do your daily meditation. Some of my clients set aside a space in their house as their proper meditation room with their specific furniture, cushions, and rugs. However, if you are just starting out, you do not need an extra meditation room. I advise to wait with this and first master the basics.

If you are a meditation beginner you may decide to meditate in your bedroom, but some of my clients have told me that they find great pleasure meditating in places like their lounge, cosy kitchen or even their zen garden or butterfly garden. The exact space where you meditate does not really matter, but it is important to start practicing your daily meditation ritual and to repeat it every day with no exceptions.

If you find that the first place you chose is not really working for you, do not be afraid to change it and choose something more spiritual. The same thing applies to the time and the meditation method that you are going to choose. If it does not work for you, just pick another possibility or another meditation technique.

As you progress in your meditation journey, you will see that the ultimate benefit of meditation is going to depend on these basics and you will be able to achieve a deep and proper mediation ritual once you got the basics down.

A beginner might find guided meditation one of the easiest ways to get started with meditation. Guided meditation contains all the instructions that you need in order to achieve a state of higher consciousness.

To get started with guided meditation all you need is a guided meditation CD or mp3 audio that you like and a place where you will not be disturbed.

Start playing the guided meditation and sit or lie down and listen to the audio instructions.

By now you should have gone through the checklist and if you do respect this checklist, you are going to achieve a proper daily meditation ritual. You are now ready to move on to the next chapter where we get started discussing the different meditation techniques.

Remember that you have to choose one meditation technique from the upcoming methods in order to achieve a proper and deep meditation ritual which in the end leads you to the ultimate meditation lifestyle!

Please proceed to the next chapters to choose which one of the meditation techniques and methods you are going to choose for your daily meditation ritual.

The Different Types Of Meditation Techniques

So what are the different types of meditation techniques?

There are many different types of meditation techniques and I will cover some of the most common and most beneficial ones throughout the upcoming chapters, but if none of the meditation techniques that I am going to cover fit your needs, you are welcome to explore the more extreme meditation methods on your own.

The internet is perfect to find out the more extreme types of meditation techniques and methods and you can get started with your research on a site called Wikipedia. Just type in the meditation method that you are looking for and you will be able to quickly find out all about it and branch out your further research from there.

Some types of meditation techniques involve just yourself and maybe a small spiritual item like a candle in order to help you focus on your meditative state.

Other types of meditation techniques do work based on guided meditation techniques like already explained in the previous chapter.

Listening to a CD or MP3 file is called guided meditation and is a good way for a beginner or get started. Again, there is no right or wrong answer and meditation comes in many forms and techniques.

Feel free to experiment with some of the types of meditation techniques that you will learn about in the upcoming chapters. Explore the different types of meditation methods until you are comfortable with one single technique.

Now, let's first look at the proper and deep breathing which is going to be covered in the next chapter and this is a very important lesson because proper and deep breathing is one of the most critical success ingredients during the meditation process.

Here we go with proper and deep breathing.

The Daily Breathing Ritual

In this chapter we will look at the proper and deep breathing exercise where you will be focusing on your breath.

This breathing technique is the basis for a proper and deep meditation.

Before choosing your meditation technique, you first have to make sure that the breathing is established because breathing correctly is part of every meditation technique that exists.

Start by adopting a comfortable position. You could sit down in a chair or lie back on a bed. The important part is to be in a comfortable position so that you are able to focus solely on your breathing activity.

Once you are comfortable, close your eyes.

Start to notice your breathing activity. We breathe in a very unconscious way and we tend to take breathing for granted.

Right now take the time to notice your breathing activity.

Notice the air filling your lungs.

Then notice as you breath out and notice the air leaving your lungs.

Repeat the breathing process and notice your breath.

As you do this, you will find thoughts coming in and going out. They might be about your personal goals, your family, your kids, your friends, your work or absolutely about anything. That does not matter. It is all part of the breathing process and it is perfectly fine to continue to have thoughts while you are in the process of meditating.

Once these incoming thoughts get noticed, just let go of them. Let them go with your next breath. The moment you notice a new thought come in, train yourself with your breathing activity and bring back your mind and only focus on your breathing in and out.

Now that we have gone through the proper and deep breathing process, let's get started with the different types of meditation techniques. The goal is to choose one of the following meditation techniques and get started with it.

It is important to go through this process right from the beginning in order to create the perfect basis for your daily meditation ritual.

If you go through this process and the checklist from above you will be able to achieve a proper and deep meditation ritual and profit from all the benefits that come with meditation.

So let's look at the next chapter where we will be discussing the first meditation technique that is called the deep walking meditation.

Walking Meditation Technique

What are the best walking meditation techniques you might ask?

If you find it difficult to sit still and keep your eyes closed while you are in the meditative state, walking meditation could be a good alternative for you.

There are four components to a successful walking meditation:

- First, you have to become aware of your breathing
- Second, you have to notice your surroundings
- Third, being conscious and attentive to your body's movement is very important
- Fourth, taking some time to reflect on your personal meditation experience is key

Become aware of your breathing in much the same way as you would for the breathing meditation process that we have been talking about in the last chapter.

Notice each breath as you are breathing in and out.

Become conscious of the air gradually filling your lungs and use each exhalation to send out any disturbing thoughts that come to mind - you will find that after a little bit of practicing this process, your extraneous thoughts will naturally find their way out of your brain on a cushion of air!

When you start being aware of your surroundings, you will likely be amazed of your awareness.

For example, when you are walking around in your home, office, the park, or any other public places, do you notice the different colors that you see?

Do you notice that even blades of grass, which initially appear just "green", are actually varied in color and hue?

You will find that once you start this tuning in process or awareness process, you will notice more and more things that have previously been ignored by your attention.

Here is a tip for you.

Do not just notice colors or listen out for sounds. For example there may be bird song or other natural sounds in the country-side, or road noise or the chatter of people and animals. Consciously make sure to tune in to these different sounds and notice the different tunes that are surrounding you.

If you are in an urban area, make sure to pay attention to the different traffic noises. Each car engine has a slightly different sound. You will find yourself being aware of certain things that have passed you by before this exercise. There are also smells to fill your senses. Maybe the aroma of freshly chopped herbs, mown grass, or the sweet smell that comes up just after a refreshing rain. There are plenty of smells in the atmosphere, but the chances are that most of these smells have slipped past your senses and consciousness.

Heck, we are taking lots of things for granted in our life and a lot of the things that are around us go completely unnoticed.

If you like the walking meditation, tune into your body's movements and senses. Start to notice the light pressure on the soles of your feet as you are walking bare feet. Be aware of the air brushing onto your skin and notice the temperature of the air and start noticing whether it is a calm day or a windy day. Pay attention to your body's movement and listen to your senses as you walk around and go through your walking meditation.

Feel how your arms swing as you walk along. Are your arms heavy or light? Notice how you hold your head - is it upright and alert or what positions are you using? Switch your attention to different body parts as you are walking around and you will be fascinated at what you will discover.

Once you've completed your walking meditation, take a small amount of time to come back to your normal day routine. During this period, mentally run through your thoughts and feelings that you have been experiencing during your walking meditation process. Think what you can do to ameliorate your experience even further next time you choose to do a walking meditation.

Gradually come back from your peaceful walking meditative state to your regular reality.

Now you are aware of the first meditation method called walking meditation and in the next chapter we are looking at another meditation technique called the healing meditation.

The Healing Meditation Technique

So what exactly do you need to know about the healing meditation technique?

You can use a healing meditation to focus on your own healing or to help with the healing of others. When you are just starting out, it is probably best to focus on your own healing, so that is what we will concentrate on first.

During a healing meditation, you can help your body to recover from an illness or disease.

Start your meditation process as usual.

Then, once you are happy that you are in a relaxed state, you can start your healing meditation.

In your mind's eye, fill the area that needs healing with a bright healing light. Once you get proficient at this healing meditation technique, you can go ahead and research online the different colors that are said to help even more with the healing process. Type into Google terms like "healing meditation colors", "colors for healing process", or any other variations.

As a starter, I recommend to use a bright white light for your healing process and visualize the area that needs healing with the bright white light and flood it with that bright white light in your mind's eye.

See everything brilliantly illuminated. The affected area should be visualized and start the healing process from there and going through the entire healing process and do this as long you see fit and until the state of entire health has mentally been achieved.

Some meditators find it very helpful to visualize their white blood cells attacking the harmful elements in the affected area, while others find that they can build their own mental construction team of miniature experts via their visualization process.

This mental construction team of miniature experts

goes for the healing process and the reconstruction of the affected area. In their mind's eye the meditators are

visualizing this construction team of miniature experts. If you like visualization you can visualize this expert team putting the ill and affected area back to a normal and healed state.

Just think about the power of this type of visualization. It is fantastic and it lets your mind do the work while you perform your healing meditation process.

You can do your visualization the following way.

Visualize the area that needs to be healed and transformed into a state of pure health. If you find it difficult to "visualize" the affected area, then just imagine what it would feel like if that affected part of your body was completely healed and in a perfect state of health.

It does not matter if you do not get all the details completely right at first. Just get a feeling of what will happen. Your mind is powerful on its own and it is so powerful that it will go ahead and fill in the gaps automatically for you - all you are helping with is telling it the direction that you would like it to go.

I hope by now you have really understood the power and benefits of the healing meditation and it is up to you to chose the right meditation technique for your own situation.

In order to find the proper meditation technique for your lifestyle, I suggest you first go through the whole guide because I am still covering other types of meditation techniques. Get a feeling of all the types of meditation techniques first and then make your final choice.

So in your quest for finding that one meditation technique that fits your own lifestyle best, let's continue with the next meditation method and that is called the Zen meditation.

The Zen Meditation Technique

How do we do the Zen meditation the proper way?

Zen meditation is normally practiced sitting on a cushion or blanket on the floor or ground if you do it outside.

In Zen meditation, there are two main items that are called Zafu and Zabuton. The Zabuton is a mat placed on the floor and the Zafu is a cushion that is placed on top of the Zabuton. Both items can help to take the pressure off your legs during Zen meditation.

The idea of using cushions during your Zen meditation sessions is to help you focus your mind on the meditation itself. Zen meditation works best if you do not feel any aches or pains that you might experience whilst sitting on a hard ground or wooden floor.

The aim of zen meditation is to simply sit and open the "hand" of thought. Traditionally, Zen meditation is practised only in a sitting position. The Zen meditator is sitting down with his or her legs and hands folded and with a spine that is kept upright during the Zen meditation.

There are several different Zen meditation sitting positions that you can take during your Zen meditation practice.

Keep checking the internet for some additional Zen meditation position illustrations if you have difficulty on your own and keep in mind that the internet might always be a good option for your meditation research.

It is especially helpful for any type of meditation illustration type of research and there are tons of inspirational and creative meditation position illustrations that you can find via research and turn them into your meditation position models.

If you type in the phrase "Zen meditation position illustrations" into Google, you will find the most inspirational Zen meditation positions.

Always remember that Google is your best friend when it comes to inspiration and creative ways to add to your collection of Zen meditation positions.

Once you have reached your desired Zen meditation sitting position, make sure to half lower your eyelids. Your eyes should not be fully open nor fully closed. This eye position will help you to stay awake and it also helps with not being distracted by outside objects that are surrounding you.

When you start the Zen meditation, you will start out by concentrating. Concentrating involves that you are going to focus your mind on your breath.

As you become more and more experienced with Zen meditation, you will find that you can concentrate and focus your mind and what took you a long time when you started out is now taking you mere seconds.

Some of my meditation students have noticed that they achieved best results with Zen meditation by joining a local Zen meditation group. They tell me about their positive experiences that they have achieved and that they have been getting the most out of the various teachings associated with Zen meditation together with the support of a Zen meditation group.

I recommend you check out your local ad section or business directory in order to find out more about joining a Zen meditation group.

You can do the research online and places like Zen meditation meetup groups in your local area might be a good start.

You can also check online places like Linked in groups that are focusing on Zen meditation or local Facebook Zen meditation Fan Pages.

Once you have done your initial online research and found an interesting zen meditation group in your area, you will be surprised what joining a local Zen meditation group can do for you.

In the next chapter we are exploring yet another meditation technique called the guided meditation technique.

The Guided Meditation Technique

In the introduction, I have already talked about the many benefits of guided meditation and pointed out that guided meditation is a good option for a meditation beginner because it is an easy way to get started.

In this chapter about guided meditation, I am going deeper and show you what guided meditation is all about so that you can decide for yourself if it is the right meditation technique for you.

Guided meditations is a good place to start your meditation practice and I recommend it to every beginner who wants to get started with meditation because it is possible and easy for a beginner to guide himself or herself through the entire meditation process.

The easiest guided meditations to follow are

pre-recorded guided meditation sessions and all you have to do is sit back and listen to the sound of the instructions.

A guided meditation will usually begin by taking you to a quiet and placid place. Some typical places that you are asked to visualize are:

A peaceful beach with the sound of the soft waves that are flooding to the shore.

A calm garden with beautiful flowers, butterflies or birds that sing and sometimes there is a river with streaming water.

A quiet forest that you enjoy with a babbling brook and the sounds of nature and wild life.

Once you are in this placid place, you will be guided to notice your senses like your feelings, sounds, smells and all the other sensations that you are going to experience during the guided meditation session.

For example, if you are in a flower/butterfly garden or forest, you will probably be guided to notice the feeling of the fresh grass that tickles your feet and the flowers that you smell.

If you are visualizing a beach scene during your guided meditation, you will be guided to notice the feeling of the warm sand and the salty breeze of the sea.

As you go through your guided meditation session, you will gradually explore the surroundings, bringing in the other sensations that you are supposed to experience as you explore the place that the guided meditation is taking you to.

You should be aware that guided meditation can be mixed with elements of hypnosis, and a hypnotic deepening routine might be used to drop your state of mind down into a meditative state of consciousness.

This hybrid guided meditation mixed with hypnosis technique is even more powerful than the less extreme guided meditation.

As you are exploring your options, be aware of the two forms of guided meditation and decide which one you want to start with.

I recommend to you as a beginner to start with the regular guided meditation and as you progress you can always add more hypnosis elements.

Do not overwhelm yourself in the beginning and do not choose a technique that is too hard to follow.

You can always do the more complicated hybrid version of the guided meditation later.

In the beginning you must stick to your daily meditation ritual and if it is too hard to do you will quit. Stick to the easiest form of the guided meditation technique first and go from there.

If you are progressing like this and stick to the instructions, you will make sure to get the best benefits out of meditation and that is the only way to go. You will achieve a deep and proper meditation ritual and you will be able to integrate your daily meditation effortlessly into your lifestyle if you follow this directions

In the next chapter we are looking at yet another meditation technique, so please make sure to proceed to the next chapter in order to complete your checklist from above.

The following chapter is an exciting one and it covers the chakra meditation technique.

The Chakra Meditation Technique

So what is chakra meditation all about and why is it so exciting?

Chakra meditation is used to energize the seven different energy centers that are located throughout your body.

These centers are:

• **Crown chakra**. The crown chakra like the name suggests is based outside your body and just above your head and this chakra is considered to be the master chakra that controls all the other chakras. The crown chakra is represented by a vilolet color.

- **Ajna or third eye chakra.** The ajna or third eye chakra is linked with your pineal gland. The pineal gland is a small gland and it is located in your brain. The color of this chakra is represented by the color indigo.
- **Throat chakra.** This chakra is linked with your thyroid gland and this chakra is represented by the color of blue.
- **Heart chakra.** The heart chakra is located at your heart and the heart chakra is linked with your immune system. Keeping your heart chakra in tune is going to help with your overall well being and health and the heart chakra is represented with a green color.
- **Solar plexus chakra.** The solar plexus chakra corresponds with your pancreas and adrenal glands. The solar plexus chakra does play a very valuable role in your digestion system and it is represented by a yellow color.
- **Sacral chakra.** The sacral chakra is located in your groin. You have to be aware that the sacral chakra is related to your emotions, your sexuality and your creativity. If the sacral chakra is out of balance you may notice mood swings. The sacral chakra is represented by an orange color.
- **Base or root chakra.** The base or root chakra is associated with your instincts that control the survival and security instincts and it is located at the base of your spine. The base chakra is represented by a red color.

How does a typical chakra meditation look like? The typical chakra meditation will start at your base or root chakra and from there it gradually works up the way through each of the other chakras until it reaches the top crown chakra.

As the meditation progresses, each chakra will be balanced and that is the goal of the chakra meditation. This type of meditation will work on each chakra in turn and it will focus on getting the body and mind balanced.

It is a fact that imbalances happen over time and chakra meditation helps balancing back the chakras into their natural state of balance and thus chakra meditation helps with the healing process of the body and a healthy mind/body connection. The goal of the chakra meditation is to move each of the different chakras until they are in a perfect balanced state with each other.

When starting out with this type of meditation, it is probably best to use a pre-recorded guided meditation that walks you through each of the chakras and that gives you guided instructions in order to ensure that the balancing process is followed by you exactly as stated by the instructions.

The chakra meditation is a very complex type of meditation and at the same time a very exciting one because it involves all the different chakras and their complexities.

In my mind it is one of the most exciting meditation methods and you can achieve great benefits if you base your daily meditation ritual on the chakra meditation.

If you like to stick with the chakra meditation, I suggest to get some additional inspiration online. If you are typing in the phrase "guided chakra meditation" or other variations of this phrase, you will be able to find some qualitative programs that will get you started with chakra meditation. From there on you can progress with your chakra meditation and gradually add some more complex chakra meditation programs to your collection as you get more experienced.

The main thing as with all the other meditation techniques is to stick with it and develop a daily meditation ritual. Once you are able to do your chakra meditation on a daily basis, you will achieve the benefits that come from this type of meditation.

If you are choosing the chakra meditation as your favorite meditation and if you are able to stick to it on a daily basis, you are going to achieve the proper and deep meditation ritual lifestyle that every meditator is aiming for.

In the next chapter we are looking at yet another meditation technique, the Christian meditation technique.

The Christian Meditation Technique

So how does the Christian meditation work the proper way?

Quite simply, Christian meditation is a type of meditation that has been placed in a Christian context.

Christian meditation goes right back to biblical times and if you are a religious person, I suggest to get started with the Christian meditation to make the process easier for you.

Any act of prayer or worship can be used to get you into a meditative state. The Bible itself states that all true Christians must meditate on the word of God.

What does this mean? This simply means that you can use some or all of your meditation exercise time to contemplate. You can contemplate about anything that relates to your spiritual or religious faith.

Christian meditation is all about clearing your mind and focusing your meditation session on worshipping God's word.

Most monks do spend most of their time in a meditative state and they have all learned to speak with God during their prayer. The clarity of the mind and consciousness that is experienced during the meditation process is going to help with this process of Christian meditation.

Some forms of Christian meditation rituals do use a mantra. A mantra is a word that is repeated during the meditation all the time. There are different mantras that can be used with Christian meditation as well.

I suggest to research these various mantras online in order to get some creative inspiration for the best mantra that you can use for yourself and one that is going to fit best with your own belief system.

Notice that Christian meditation has nothing to do with clearing you from your sins. Christian meditation does not replace the religious process of being absolved from one's sins.

Christian meditation is a very useful tool that many Christians apply in order to develop a stronger relationship with the word of God.

In the next chapter we are looking at yet another meditative way that you can practice during your daily meditation ritual.

So let's go ahead and look at the Japan meditation techniques.

The Japan Meditation Technique

So what are the proper Japan meditation techniques?

Like the Christian meditation, the Japan meditation involves the repetition of a mantra during the course of the meditation process.

The mantra is usually spoken in a very soft and low voice and only the person that actually is chanting the mantra can hear it. It is very rare that the mantra is repeated in the meditator's mind during the Japan meditation.

The Japan meditation is often practiced while the meditator is sitting in a yogic meditation position. Sitting down in a comfortable meditation position and reciting a mantra is the normal course of the Japan meditation. There are situations where the meditator lies down in a meditation position as well.

The most popular Japan mantras are the following:

If you are practicing Buddhist and Hindu meditation traditions or transcendental meditation, you will be receiving your mantra by your personal meditation guru.

The goal of the mantra is varied and it depends on the type of meditation that you are practicing.

The mantra is often a simple personal communication with God and can be compared to in a similar way to prayer.

Once you have been going through the Japan meditation method, you are now ready to move on to the next meditation technique that is called the new age meditation technique.

The New Age Meditation Technique

So how do we do the new age meditation the proper way?

Many meditators, myself included, do find that the easiest way to meditate is to simply sit or lie back and listen to the pre-recorded sound of a new age meditation audio.

There are plenty of meditation audio programs out there to choose from. I will also be covering some of the best meditation programs, including new age meditation audio programs.

I will be discussing these at the end of this guide in a separate section and I am only including meditation programs that have been tried, proven, and tested by myself and my students.

Let's talk about new age meditation. Did you know that new age meditation can also take the form of a background track. This happens usually in the form of a rainfall or some other natural sounds.

Behind this rainfall or natural sound track, the brain is exposed to some other sounds called binaural beats or some other tones.

These "binaural beats" and other type of new age tones are designed to induce a natural meditative state and all of this really happens without any of the hard work that normally goes into the traditional meditation process.

Some traditional meditators consider the new age meditation cheating. Personally, I find it the quickest and easiest way to make meditation work because new age meditation represents our modern lifestyle.

All you need to know about new age meditation is the following. Sit or lie down in a comfortable meditative position and place your headphones on your ears and listen to the sounds.

The pre-recorded new age meditation track does all the rest for you.

My favorite of these types of pre-recorded new age meditation programs is the Centerpointe Holosync system, which can be found at Centerpointe.com.

I personally use this new age meditation system every evening after a nice walk outside with a loved one, and after having taken a nice warm shower and a cup of herbal meditation tea, and before I go to sleep.

The Centerpointe Holosync system has a number of different levels that you can choose from and which take you deeper and deeper and into your highest level of meditative state. I have been using this system for a number of years and have noticed lots of positive changes as I am progressing and going through my daily meditation ritual.

I have tried out almost all of the most popular meditation techniques in order to be able to understand the differences and similarities of all of them, but since I have been adding the new age meditation method to my inventory, I have noticed that I have become generally calmer and more relaxed as opposed to the other more traditional meditation techniques.

I am applying a mix of more than one meditation methods, but the new age meditation that I am practicing before bed time is one of my favorite meditation techniques, and since I have been actively applying this easy to use new age method to my evening meditation process, I feel totally in tune with myself.

I like it so much because, if for some reason I am not able to do my morning meditation, I am still able to fulfill my daily meditation ritual requirements. No matter how tired I feel after a hard day of work, I am still able to do my daily meditation ritual with this new age meditation technique and I am able to do it because this meditation technique is so easy and effortless to apply.

This is my secret meditation method and this is how I am able to achieve a daily meditation ritual lifestyle every day of the week!

Heck, even if I am very tired after a long day of work and have not been able to do any of my other day time meditation techniques, I still achieve my daily meditation ritual with this genius meditation method.

The deep and proper meditation ritual lifestyle that I enjoy living requires me to at least practice one type of daily meditation exercise. If you like you can refer back to my checklist to revise the criteria for a proper and deep meditation ritual lifestyle.

Using the new age meditation method helps me achieve my goal.

Don't get me wrong here. I am not only practicing this one effortless new age meditation technique as the only method of meditation. No way!

However, if there is no time left before I have to get to sleep, or if I am already too tired for doing anything else, this is a wonderful and effortless method.

It is wonderful because I am getting done my daily meditation exercise and thus am able to enjoy a lifestyle that includes meditation! This method has allowed me to achieve a true meditation lifestyle which would not have been possible without this method and this is why I call the program of this book "The Daily Meditation Ritual Lifestyle".

Without this new age meditation method my program would not work because there are many days of the week where I am just not able to apply a more traditional meditation method.

It is kind of my secret method and the reason why I am able to achieve a daily meditation ritual lifestyle or a life that includes meditation on a daily basis.

In my opinion achieving a true meditation lifestyle is the only way to go in order to enjoy life in the most beneficial way.

The new age meditation technique has enabled me to lead this awesome meditation lifestyle that I would not want to miss for just a single day.

Now you know my true secret ingredient for achieving the ultimate meditation lifestyle. It is so powerful and effortless and this is why it works and has never failed me once. I do not consider this cheating but this is a method that automatically fulfills the requirements that have to be fulfilled for leading a daily meditation ritual and a lifestyle with meditation!

A lifestyle with meditation in turn will bring you great joy, happiness, health, energy, and unlimited possibilities and this is why respecting the rules and guidelines of my program "The Daily Meditation Ritual Lifestyle" are so critical.

You can achieve this goal of a meditation lifestyle by including the new age meditation into your day if you are short in time.

Use this secret shortcut anytime you need to and as often as you need to and if you do so your success with this program is going to be guaranteed because you are following the guidelines.

Do not skip the daily meditation ritual for one day.

If you have no time left before going to sleep just replace your choosen meditation technique that you usually apply with the new age meditation technique.

If you follow these instructions, you are going to be able to lead the ultimate meditation lifestyle that will bring you unlimited benefits on all levels!

Here you have it, the new age meditation is the success ingredient and the reason why this program works so well!

The new age meditation can be done on a daily basis and everyone can take at least 5 minutes out of his or her day or before bed time and listen to a new age audio program without taking any mental effort.

This is the perfect method for a beginner to achieve a meditation lifestyle in no time.

This is the perfect method for an advanced meditator to improve or add the secret sauce that turns meditation into a true meditation lifestyle.

This is the perfect method for someone who loves meditation but lacks time.

Let's recap and repeat why this method is so powerful for anyone who practises meditation.

My checklist from above requires a daily meditation practice. This requirement is easily fulfilled with the new age meditation technique because it can easily be repeated on a daily basis because everyone can spare at least 5 minutes out of the day and follow an effortless audio program.

This is a great method for those who are really busy because the new age meditation technique helps everyone achieve a daily meditation ritual and thus a true meditation lifestyle.

Everyone who is thinking that a lifestyle that includes a daily meditative process might be impossible because of time constraints is advised to rethink this because the new age meditation technique makes a lifestyle with meditation possible.

Heck, everyone who applies my checklist together with this new age meditation technique is going to achieve a daily meditation ritual. A daily meditation ritual is the basis for creating a meditation lifestyle which is the ultimate goal of this program!

Why?

Because a proper meditation lifestyle is going to bring you the most valuable benefits on all levels. You are going to lead a happier, healthier and more enjoyable life and everything that you want is going to happen!

All you have to do is apply the daily meditation ritual the proper way and as instructed in this program.

You should by now be able to choose one meditation technique from all the meditation techniques that are covered in the guide and make active use of the new age meditation technique whenever you need it or lack time.

There are no more excuses why you are not able to accomplish the daily meditation ritual because the new age meditation only takes 5 minutes and takes no effort on your part.

Please take some time now and evaluate what specific meditation technique you are going to choose as your main meditation method and replace it with the new age meditation method whenever you need it.

Get started with the daily meditation ritual today!

You can revise the Daily Meditation Ritual guidelines once again and go through the checklist below:

• Choose one of the meditation methods from one of the
meditation technique chapters

• Choose a time of day (morning, lunch, afternoon, evening) when you are not going to be inerrupted. Make sure to repeat your meditation on a daily basis.

• Choose a placid place where you feel cosy, comfortable and where you can relax.

• Replace your choosen meditation technique with the new age meditation technique whenever you need or for whatever reason. Just do it!

Just stick to these 4 simple rules and you will achieve a proper and deep meditation ritual and with it the ultimate meditation lifestyle.

Conclusion

I do not let one day pass without practising my daily meditation ritual and this is why I call this guide "The Daily Meditation Ritual Lifestyle".

Hopefully by now this program has shown you how to achieve this meditation ritual lifestyle for yourself.

Once you are able to stick to the checklist, you will be able to live this ultra valuable meditation lifestyel for yourself.

This is the true mediation lifestyle that every meditator wants to achieve.

In this program you have been going through the basic questions like what is meditation and how to get started.

Once the basic questions have been clarified, I gave you a checklist with 4 specific guidelines to follow.

I then asked you to go through the rest of the program and do your own evaluation work and choose the one meditation technique that you like to get started with and that is the most appropriate for your personal situation.

Hopefully by now you are able to find out which meditation technique is the most appropriate for you so that you can get started with it today.

Please do not delay and once you have identified your preferred meditation technique do get started with your meditation work ASAP!

To get started with the meditation work, go back to the specific chapter where the mediation technique that you have chosen by now is explained in detail.

Set aside at least 5 minutes per day and follow the instructions within the specific chapter.

Follow the guidelines to the T without any exceptions (daily repetition of meditation for at least 5 minutes per day, place or space where you feel comfortable, choose one meditation technique that you like and follow instructions, replace with new age meditation if needed).

Throughout the guide I have also explained to you what meditation technique is best for a meditation beginner and why.

I have explained why the new age meditation technique is my secret ingredient and if you skipped this chapter, please go back to the new age meditation chapter right now because I reveal a huge take away for everybody who is busy and thinks meditation does not work for them.

You know by now that you can also add some of your own creativity into your choosen meditation technique.

I talked about some fun and exciting ways to spice up your meditation ritual and told you that you can start using a hybrid version of your traditional meditation technique

As long as you stick to the daily meditation ritual rules and guidelines you are fine and you can add some of your own creative add ons from your own meditation collection.

Remeber to use Google as a tool if you want to come up with some creative and inspirational illustrations for meditation positions and mantras that you need for your choosen meditation technique.

By now you have finished the program and if you are getting started following the 4 easy to follow guidelines today, you will very soon reap the benefits of a true meditation lifestyle.

Congratulations and welcome to the Ultimate Meditation Lifestyle!

One More Thing & Final Words

We all have room for improvement of our meditation process and therefore we need to learn the proper and deep meditation routine.

Just follow this guide and you are going to achieve this goal. If you are going to use this guide and take action on a daily basis, you will achieve the ultimate meditation lifestyle together with the many benefits that come with it.

In order to get the most benefit out of this guide, make sure to go through the checklist, your own evaluation process, and the different types of meditation techniques that are covered in this guide.

If neccessary go through the guide a second time and do the evaluation work. Once you are done, choose one single meditation technique that you like and get started with the instructions the same day and do not procrastinate.

If you do this the way that I have instructed you to do it, you will achieve unlimited benefits for almost no work and I guess this is the huge valuable lesson that you can take away from this program.

Make sure to do your meditation work every day because you will only achieve the benefits if you apply the guidelines that are mentioned in the checklist above.

Once you get the simplicity of what I am teaching you here and once you are able to do your daily meditation work, you will have achieved the daily meditation routine in a proper, easy and effortless way...

"Welcome to the Ultimate Meditation Lifestyle"

Meditation Resources & Tips

This is the list of my own recommended and proven meditation programs that I have been mentioning to you in a previous chapter.

There is a range of guided meditation programs that you can download instantly. They include relaxation, creating abundance in your life, enhancing your creativity and connecting with your higher self. You can download these types of programs for free online and you can do a simple search to find them. Just type in search phrases like the ones above into Google.

You can also type in search phrases like the individual chapter titles from this book, for example, new age meditation technique, new age meditation audio, zen meditation technique, or japan meditation mantra and Google will give you the results.

In order to complete your meditation knowledge, you can start building your personal library of meditation documentation, depending on your preferences. Doing this research is a fun, inspirational, creative, stimulating, and educational process.

Today there are a lot of new age meditation type of games and apps available for you to tap into. These are all great resources and devices that can help you out with managing your daily meditation ritual.

You can gradually add them to your repertoire or use them in conjunction with what you are already doing on a daily basis. You can start exploring these new media types of meditation programs as you are progressing.

Just do a quick search for terms like "meditation", "meditation time management", "meditation positions", "meditation mantras", "new age meditation audio", "relaxation music", "zen music", "holistic music", "new age music", etc. and you will be surprised what you will find. Be creative with your search terms and you are going to be in for a real treat!

You can also do a search for the phrases and chapter titles that I have been using througout this guide and just add the word music, audio, pre-recorded, mp3, or program to the end of each phrase and type your search string like this into Google or the App marketplaces.

Be creative with your search terms because the more creative you are the better results you are going to get back.

You will find the most recent and most up to date type of meditation programs in all kinds of ways, shapes, or forms and searching all types of marketplaces and search engines will reveal the best information.

I recently came across a new search engine that searches a multitude of marketplaces and search engines simultaneously as you type in the search term and this might be a wonderful way to get your search project started. The search engine is called Soovle.com.

Apple apps are very popular and if you are a mobile person, I recommend to search the Apple App store and the Google Android marketplace at Google Play for some killer meditation apps.

Meditation apps are not only fun but also help you get organized because you can set a timer for the recommended 5 to 20 minutes that are required for your daily meditation time and you can time your meditation like this.

There are many other functions in a meditation app that you might find helpful as a meditator so make sure to check out all your options with meditation apps.

I have recently created my own meditation app called the Meditation Helper for Your Daily Ritual and you can find it either via the Google Play Store (just type in Google Play into Google to find it). Once at Google Play just type in the search phrase Meditation Helper & Trainer to find it.

Just look at the bottom right hand side and you can check it out from there. This app will show you some functionality so that you can see the possibilities and what an app can do for you.

There are many more advanced meditation apps out there that make the impossible possible and you will get lots of value and usability out of them if you are using them in a strategically way that benefits your daily meditation ritual.

There are also meditation games for the most common game platforms like xbox and playstation. Recently meditation guru Deepak Chopra has created his own meditation game for the Xbox called Leela and this is a wonderful option for younger people or for people who love technology and games to get in touch with their mind and achieve the ultimate mind body connection.

The program is designed to create a mental, emotional and spiritual balance. The main thing is to experience the body and mind with Leela. As Deepak Chopra puts it himself: "The main thing is to experience your body and mind with Leela and have fun and let go and flow and if you let go and flow you let go and flow with life".

In order to achieve the best results with the new age meditation technique, I recommend the Centerpointe Holosync high tech meditation system. I highly recommend it because not only have I tested it myself with great success, but some of my meditation students achieved the same positive results with the system.

This is the absolute dream come true and makes your daily meditation ritual easy and effortlessly.

This is my secret ingredient for being able to achieve my own Daily Meditation Ritual Lifestyle! Please refer back to the New Age Meditation chapter where you can get more details on this secret meditation technique and why it is so valuable.

The system works like this. Just put a CD into your player, put on your headphones and press "play". Let the Holosync system take care of taking you to a level of meditation rarely experienced unless you are a Zen monk.

I highly urge you to go though the guide and take action and live the daily meditation ritual starting now!

To your **Meditation Lifestyle** success

Did you love *Daily Meditation Beginner's Guide From Happines & Good Life to Stress Release, Relaxation, Healing, Weight Loss & Zen*? Then you should read *Meditation Book For Beginners: 15 Daily Strenght Training & Home Workout Yoga Routines For Beginning Yogi Students* by Juliana Baltimoore!

Meditation Book For Beginners: 15 Daily Strenght Training & Home Workout Yoga Routines For Beginning Yoga Studentsis a book that is well timed. This meditation and mindfulness book explores all the aspects of Yoga that an individual that is interested in starting a daily Yoga routine would want to know about. This spiritual meditation book takes the reader via fifteen+ short and fun lessons and exercises through the various aspects of a proper Yoga lifestyle.The meditation book goes step by step starting with the most fascinating and intriguing aspects and types of Yoga techniques that a beginning Yogi can choose from like Bikram Yoga, Hatha Yoga, Ashtanga Yoga, and many more and the last lesson ends with Yoga For Busy Yoga Beginners.The process of Yoga is still a mystery to man in the Western World due to religious reasons. As things have become more integrated however, more and more Western people are becoming exposed and fascinated by Yoga and are curious to learn where it all started and how it can be beneficial to the daily life. The book gives the novice Yoga student just enough information to enable him or her to make an informed decision as to whether or not a Yoga routine might be a healthy lifestyle decision. Combine Yoga with a light and healthy food choice and a daily Yoga ritual will become the most powerful and enjoyable lifestyle. Once you do apply this daily Yoga routine you will become a warrior and you will command and receive the unlimited health benefits that are possible with such a daily Yoga lifestyle choice. There are some great nuggets about Yoga & Cures for Diseases like Asthma, High Blood Pressure & Diabetes that someone who is suffering from might look for via a healthy living & workout solution with Yoga. Why This Book? Thanks to media and press about this book, Yoga has made quite a comeback in recent years as more and more individuals start to realize the many benefits that they can accrue from doing this low impact form of exercise. Yoga & Meditation instructors can tell because they are getting all these beginner questions like: "What are the true benefits of Yoga?" "What is Tantra Yoga?", "What Are Your Experiences From Dru Yoga?", "What Is Drishti Yoga?", "Can I Cure Hight Blood Pressure Via Yoga?", "Are Cures Of Health Issues Realistic Via Yoga?", "I Am Busy Can I Do It, Too?" "How to do yoga at home?", "How to do yoga at home for beginners?", "What are the best Yoga positions for beginners?", "What are the best Yoga routines for beginners to get started with for Yoga beginners?", etc. This is how the idea of this meditation guide was born. The book is designed to answer all the questions and shed light on everything that a beginner should know about the wonderful and fascinating world of Yoga. There are other books that talk about Yoga for beginning students, but the focus of this book is different because it does not talk about a certain Yoga topic in a boring, drawn out and long winded way, but it gives you a quick and snappy lesson to read and enjoy and to move on and encourage you to take action. To make the reading process insightful and inspirational there are also some fascinating facts and stories included about curing Asthma and breathing problems with Yoga. If you are suffering from any health problem looking into the chapter 14 is going to answer many questions for you. This beginning Yoga book is not expensive as opposed to high prized Yoga trainers plus this book makes reading on your device very personal, enjoyable & inspirational. Get your copy today & achieve a toxin free & zen body and mind!

Also by Juliana Baltimoore

Meditation Book For Beginners: 15 Daily Strength Training & Home Workout Yoga Routines For Beginning Yogi Students

Daily Meditation Beginner's Guide From Happines & Good Life to Stress Release, Relaxation, Healing, Weight Loss & Zen

Daily Yoga Routine Beginner's Guide For Happiness The Mindful & Healthy Lifestyle With Zen & Spiritual Eternity

Daily Meditation Eternity Prayer Poem Book For Positve Mindset, Motivation, Happiness, Success, Health & Relationships

Superfoods Recipes: Chicken Soup Recipes For Cold Recovery, Healthy Chicken Noodle Soup Recipes, Holistic Healing Chicken Recipes & Homemade Healing Noodle Soup With Chicken

31 Blender & Mixer Smoothie Recipes For Rapid Weight Loss

The Poetry Book For The Paleo Lifestyle

21 Green Fruit And Vegetable Smoothie Snacks: Green Fruit Yogurt Smoothies, Vegan Desserts & Herbal Veggie Bullet Blender Drinks

Blender Cookbook: 60 Blender Cocktails Recipes For Body Cleanse & Detox, Energy, Vitality & Rapid Weight Loss

Fasting Book For Health, Fitness, Weight Loss & Detoxing 11 Juicing For Beginners Recipes With delicious & Healthy Fruit & Vegetable Juices

Juicing Recipes Book For Vitality, Energy, Health And Fitness Nutrition 14 Healthy Clean Eating & Drinking Juice Cleanse Recipes

Smoothie Recipe Book To Gain Energy & Detox 17 Smoothie Bowl Recipes, Cleanse Drinks & Blender Mix Recipes To Feel Stronger

Fitness Cookbook: 60 Healthy Nutrition Blender Recipes, Vegan Gourmet Recipes, Juicing Drinks, Dessert Recipes & Healthy Ice Creams For Wellness, Health & Happiness

Juicing Recipe Book: 27 Epic Juice & Blender Recipes For Health, Detox, Weight Loss, Energy, Strength & Vitality

Scrumptious Paleo Desserts: Low Fat Low Cholesterol Dessert Recipes For A Healthy, Happy, Lean & Clean Eating Lifestyle

Weight Loss Juicing Recipe Book: Epic Juicer Mixer Blender Recipes For Loosing Body Fat, Body Cleansing & Detox

About the Publisher

InfinitYou is a hybrid general interest trade publisher. One of the first of its kind InfinitYou publishes physical books, electronic books, and audiobooks in various genres. Our publications are meant to educate, edify and entertain readers of all walks of life from babies to the elderly. Home to more than twenty imprints such as Infinit Baby, Infinit Kids, Infinit Girl, Infinit Boy, Infinit Coloring, Infinit Swear Words, Infinit Activities, Infinit Productivity, Infinit Cat, Infinit Dog, Infinit Love, Infinit Family, Infinit Survival, Infinit Health, Infinit Beauty, Infinit Spirituality, Infinit Lifestyle, Infinit Wealth, Infinit Romance, and lots more.

www.ingramcontent.com/pod-product-compliance
Lightning Source LLC
LaVergne TN
LVHW012130070526
838202LV00056B/5938